Contents

Chapter 1   The Roman Empire   4
Looking at Roman art   6

Chapter 2   The story of Rome   8
The republic   10
Conquering the empire   12
Civil wars   14
The image of Augustus   16

Chapter 3   The city of Rome   18
Roman architecture   20
Sculpture   22
Public shows   24
Trade and crafts   26

Chapter 4   Family life   28
House and garden   30
Mosaics   32
Burying the dead   34

Chapter 5   Roman religion   36
Emperor worship   38
New gods   40
Christianity   42

Timeline   44
Glossary   46
Further resources   47
Index   48

Words included in the glossary are in **bold** the first time they appear in each chapter.

The Roman Empire

Art provides us with a rich source of information about life in the past. No ancient civilization has left us more art, spread over a wider area, than that of Rome. At its height, in the 2nd century AD, the Roman **Empire** included all the lands around the Mediterranean Sea, and stretched from Britain in the north to North Africa in the south, and from Spain in the west to Iraq in the east. This vast area included a population of around a hundred million people.

Romanization

The Romans encouraged the many different peoples within the empire to follow a similar way of life – to worship Roman gods, wear Roman clothes and speak the Latin language. Across the empire, people used the same coins and ate from the same types of tableware. Art and **architecture** were also used to create a uniform Roman identity. If you travelled to any Roman town, you would see similar statues and temples. The homes of the rich would be decorated with the same types of wall painting, following fashions set in Rome.

▼ The Arc de Triomphe du Carrousel in Paris is a copy of a Roman arch. It was built in 1805–6 by the French emperor, Napoleon Bonaparte, to commemorate his armies' victories.

Napoleon rides a chariot, like a victorious Roman general

The chariot was originally pulled by ancient Roman bronze horses, which Napoleon took from Venice. These have now been returned and replaced with replicas

Statues of French soldiers

Fine sandstone, brought all the way from Italy

Victoria, winged Roman goddess of victory

Columns made of red marble from southern France

A triumphal arch was both a monument and a ceremonial entrance, used for victory processions

Napoleon's arch is a copy of a Roman arch, built in AD 203 by Emperor Septimius Severus

The legacy of Rome

We are still influenced in countless ways by the ancient Romans. We use the Roman alphabet and follow a calendar with months named after Roman gods and rulers. March, for example, is named after the war god Mars. Our coins, with portraits of rulers in profile, surrounded by Latin words, are similar to Roman coins. Many of our customs, including birthday parties and major festivals, are Roman in origin. All over Europe, we still live in cities, such as Paris and London, originally built by the Romans.

From the late 18th century, architects in Europe and the USA imitated **Classical** architecture. Many public buildings, such as libraries and town halls, were based on Roman temples, with rows of columns (a style that the Romans themselves copied from the Greeks). In the 19th century, when European nations conquered their own empires, they copied Roman victory monuments, setting up triumphal arches, such as the Arc de Triomphe in Paris and Marble Arch in London. Bronze statues of kings, queens and generals on horseback are also Classical in origin.

▼ Birmingham's town hall, built in 1832–49, is based on three surviving columns of a ruined temple, dedicated to Castor and Pollux, in Rome.

▼ In 1447–50, the Italian artist Donatello made this huge bronze equestrian statue, the first large-scale bronze work to be made since Roman times. He was inspired by the statue of Emperor Marcus Aurelius (see page 6).

He holds a baton of command in his raised right hand

Erasmo da Narni (1370–1443), known as 'Gattamelata' (the Honeyed Cat), a Venetian general

The horse is a copy of Roman bronze horses in Venice

The cathedral of Padua

Winning hearts and minds

The historian Tacitus described how his father-in-law, Agricola, governor of Britain, turned the recently conquered Britons into Romans:
*'Agricola gave private encouragement and official assistance to the building of temples, public squares and good houses … Furthermore, he trained the sons of the chiefs in the liberal arts … The result was that in place of loathing the Latin language they became eager to speak it effectively. In the same way, our national dress came into favour and the **toga** was everywhere to be seen.'*

5

Looking at Roman art

We can learn a lot about the Romans from their art. Sculpture and paintings, for example, show us details of dress and hairstyles. We will learn even more if we try to work out why a piece of art was made, and how it would have been seen by an ancient Roman.

Emperor on horseback

In Rome today, you can see a 3.5-metre high bronze statue of the Emperor Marcus Aurelius riding a horse. When new, it was covered in gold leaf, though only faint traces now remain. Glittering in the sun, it must have been a spectacular sight.

Clues

To understand what this statue meant to its original viewers, we have to look for clues, like a detective. One clue is the emperor's long cloak, called a *paludamentum*. This was worn only in wartime by army commanders. Another clue comes from a 12th-century guidebook to Rome, which records that the work once included another figure: a **barbarian**, or foreign enemy of Rome. He lay beneath the horse's raised hoof, begging for his life. The figure, now missing, explains why the emperor has his right arm outstretched with his hand open. This gesture, often made by emperors in Roman art, meant the offering of mercy to a defeated enemy. So the statue was supposed to show that Marcus Aurelius was both a victorious general and a merciful ruler.

▼ This statue of Marcus Aurelius is thought to have been made soon after his death in AD 180, when he was declared to have become a god.

The rider was identified as Marcus Aurelius thanks to his coin portraits, which show the same long face with curly hair and beard

Arm outstretched, showing mercy to the defeated

The paludamentum (military cloak) shows us that the emperor is a general

Traces of gold leaf

Veins stand out on the legs

The statue shows us what Roman saddles looked like, with layers of leather cut to give decorative edges

The emperor has no stirrups, for these had not yet been invented

A fallen figure once lay here

How did it survive?

Bronze equestrian (horse-rider) statues of emperors were common sights in every Roman city. Yet the statue of Marcus Aurelius is the only complete example to survive. The rest were all melted down for their valuable metal. The reason it survived is that the pope, who kept the statue in his palace garden, wrongly thought it was of the first Christian emperor, Constantine, and so it was protected by the Church.

The original statue of Trajan was removed in the Middle Ages. This statue, of St Peter, was placed on top in 1587, by Pope Sixtus V

Trajan's column

A wonderful source for evidence about the Roman Army is a 38-metre high stone column, set up in Rome by the Emperor Trajan. This is covered with carvings showing Trajan's troops on campaign. Thanks to these carvings, we can see how Roman soldiers marched, built camps, crossed rivers and fought battles. Yet the main purpose of the column was not to record military information, but to celebrate Emperor Trajan, whose statue originally stood on top and who appears in many of the scenes, giving orders and encouraging his men. After his death, Trajan's ashes were placed in the base of the column, now his tomb.

Both Marcus Aurelius' statue and Trajan's column were made to impress the people of Rome with their ruler. Today we call such work **propaganda** – art intended to push a political message across.

◄ Trajan's column is decorated with a long spiral frieze, with reliefs showing two wars that the emperor fought in Dacia (modern Romania).

The shaft is made of nineteen drums of Italian marble, each weighing around 32 tonnes

◄ This scene from Trajan's column shows the army travelling along a river in warships known as biremes, so-called because of their two rows of oars, one above the other (*bi* means two).

The story of Rome

One of the oldest surviving works of Roman art, dating from around 500 BC, is a bronze she-wolf. The she-wolf, which also appeared on Roman coins, plays a key role in a legend about Rome's beginnings. According to this legend, the city's founder and first king, Romulus, had been abandoned as a baby along with his twin brother, Remus, and suckled by a wolf.

The twins were sons of the war god Mars. The historian Livy wrote, 'If any nation deserves the privilege of claiming a **divine** ancestry, it is our own. The glory won by the Roman people in their wars is so great that, when they declare that Mars himself was their first parent, all nations of the world should accept their claim.' In fact, **archaeology** shows that Rome had much humbler beginnings, as a scattered group of villages, in the 10th or 9th century BC, which slowly grew into a town.

▼ The bronze she-wolf stood on Rome's Capitoline Hill, the most sacred part of the city.

The she-wolf is shown in a protective attitude, looking around her with her ears pricked up

Her ribs stand out, showing that she has gone hungry in order to stay with the babies

The figures of Romulus and Remus were added in the 15th century

Greek influence

In southern Italy, there were cities founded by the Greeks, such as Paestum and Naples. The Greeks influenced both the Etruscans and the Romans, who imitated their **architecture** and sculpture. The Romans copied the three orders (styles) of Greek temples, known as Doric, Ionic and Corinthian. Doric temples, such as those at Paestum, were characterized by sturdy plain columns. The more delicate Ionic order had columns with raised narrow bands, topped by a pair of scrolls. The most decorative order was the Corinthian, which had columns topped with acanthus leaves.

◄ The temple of the goddess Hera, at Paestum in southern Italy, was built in about 550 BC. It is one of the best preserved Greek temples anywhere.

Latins and Etruscans

The Romans were just one of the Latin-speaking peoples living in western Italy, in the area known as Latium. From the 8th century BC, the greatest influence on Latium were the Etruscans, whose civilization dominated northern Italy. The Etruscans lived in wealthy cities, ruled by kings. They were experts at bronze **casting**, particularly figures of animals.

The Romans adopted many Etruscan customs, such as the wearing of a robe called a **toga**. In the 6th century, Rome was ruled by a series of kings of Etruscan descent, the last of whom was driven out in the year 510 or 509 BC.

▼ This Etruscan sarcophagus (stone coffin) shows a ceremony called a *conclamatio* (shouting together) a custom used by Greeks, Etruscans and Romans when mourning their dead.

Better than the Greeks?

When it came to art, the Romans always felt inferior to the Greeks. At the same time, they were proud that they had been able to unite the previously disunited Greeks by bringing them into their **empire**. In *The Aeneid*, the Roman poet Virgil contrasted the 'arts' of foreign peoples, such as Greeks, with those of Rome:

'There will be others to beat the breathing bronze with greater skill and grace. Others too will draw out living faces from the marble ... But you, Roman, must remember that you have to guide the nations by your authority. These are your arts: to bring the ways of peace, to show mercy to the conquered, and to crush the proud.'

The mourners cry out the name of the dead woman

They hold flasks of perfumed oil, which they use to anoint the dead

The body is laid out on a couch

Even the dog is in mourning for its mistress

The republic

After the last Etruscan king was driven out, around 509 BC, Rome's government became a **republic**. Instead of being ruled by a king, Rome was governed by annually elected officials, called **magistrates**. The most important were the two chief magistrates called **consuls**. They were Rome's heads of state, and the commanders of the armies. The consuls ruled with the advice of an assembly of approximately 600 serving and former magistrates, called the **Senate**.

Magistrates were attended in public by officials called *lictors*, who carried a bundle of rods with an axe in the middle, called a *fasces*. Originally an Etruscan symbol, this showed the power of the magistrate to punish offenders with death or a beating.

Voting

Every adult male **citizen** had the right to vote for the magistrates. Yet the work of a magistrate was unpaid, so only the wealthiest could afford to stand for election. Rich families were also able to use their influence to get their candidates elected. As a result, most of the magistrates came from only a small number of wealthy families. Women, non-citizens and slaves did not have the right to vote or hold public office.

▼ A carved relief from around 100 BC shows a census being carried out. This was the updating of the register of citizens, to determine who had the right to vote, and what taxes people should pay.

The censor, a senior magistrate, records the names of citizens

This man, identified as a citizen by his toga, has to state his name, age, occupation, amount of property and the name of his father

He carries a document, perhaps a grant of citizenship

Shirt of mail (iron rings). The plate armour shown on Trajan's column had not yet been invented

This Roman soldier provides good evidence for the armour worn in 100 BC

Toga

The toga, which could be worn only by male citizens, was a large semi-circle of cloth, around 7 metres long and 3 metres wide. Sculptures of men in togas help us work out how it was worn, draped in complicated folds around the body, covering the left arm while leaving the right arm free.

The usual toga was made of undyed wool. A toga *praetexta*, with a purple border, was worn by certain magistrates and boys from noble familes, while a black toga *pulla* was worn for funerals. Men standing for election wore a toga *candida*, whitened with chalk, which gives us our word 'candidate'. Generals in triumphal processions wore a purple toga *picta*, embroidered with gold palm leaves. Beneath the toga a Roman wore a tunic which, in the case of senators, was decorated with a broad purple stripe.

Although it was heavy and awkward, wearing a toga was a sign of respectability, like a suit and tie today. When foreigners were granted Roman citizenship, one of the first things they had to do was to learn how to wear a toga.

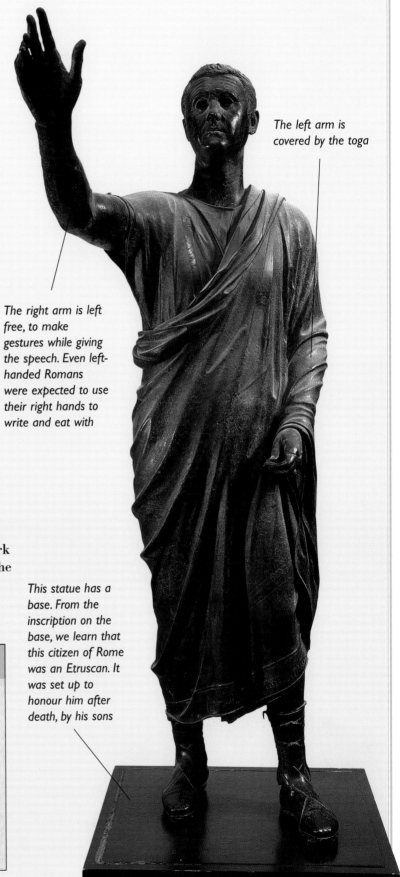

The left arm is covered by the toga

The right arm is left free, to make gestures while giving the speech. Even left-handed Romans were expected to use their right hands to write and eat with

This statue has a base. From the inscription on the base, we learn that this citizen of Rome was an Etruscan. It was set up to honour him after death, by his sons

▶ The custom of wearing a toga meant a great deal of work for ancient sculptors, forced to recreate every fold of the cloth. This bronze statue, dating from 90 BC, shows a magistrate called Aulus Metellus making a speech.

A Roman career

In the 1st century BC, the life of a Roman politician followed a set path, called the *cursus honorum* (path of honour). After spending his 20s in the army, at the age of 30, a man could stand for election as a *quaestor*. There were 20 *quaestors*, responsible for collecting taxes and spending public money. The next stage, at the age of 39, was to be made a *praetor*, one of Rome's dozen or more judges. At the age of 42, a man could stand for the consulship, the highest honour available to any Roman.

Conquering the empire

The Roman Empire was conquered little by little. From 400 to 270 BC, the Romans fought wars against other Italian peoples, eventually becoming the dominant power in the country. Rome was then drawn into three wars with the people of Carthage, in North Africa, whose own empire included Sicily and southern Spain. Carthage was finally defeated and destroyed in 146 BC. In the same period, Roman armies were campaigning in the east, conquering Greece and Syria.

The conquests in the east led to vast amounts of booty being brought back to Rome. This included many famous Greek paintings and statues, carried in triumphal processions and then used to decorate temples and other public buildings.

▼ This is just one small scene from Trajan's column, yet it is packed with information. It tells us about the Roman Army, and also about the enemy Dacians, one of whom can be seen at the bottom left.

Roman armies

Success in warfare was due to the **discipline** and skill of the legionaries – citizen soldiers who wore heavy armour and fought on foot. Each legionary carried a large shield and a short stabbing sword, called a *gladius*. The soldiers trained to march and fight in tight ranks, obeying signals from trumpeters. They followed **standard** bearers who carried golden eagles and other religious symbols, on long poles. These were treated as sacred objects, which it was a disgrace to lose in battle.

Like soldiers in modern armies, Roman soldiers dressed alike, wearing red tunics beneath their identical armour. The shields of each legion were decorated with the same images, such as thunderbolts and eagles. This helped the men think of themselves as a group, rather than individuals, and made them better fighters.

The figures march up the column, from left to right. It is as if the column is a mountain, which the army is climbing

This line shows where two of the column's drums joined together. This shows that the carving was done after the column was erected

The helmets have small rings on top, so they could be hung from a cord over the shoulder when they were not worn

A captured Dacian, with beard, cloak and long trousers

The standards were decorated with various images, including wreaths (prizes for victory) and portraits of the emperor

This standard with a square flag on top was called a vexillum. It carried the legion's number and name

The shields are decorated with eagles' wings and lightning bolts, both emblems of Jupiter, the sky god and protector of Rome

The men's big muscles show how fit they were, due to constant exercise such as long marches carrying heavy equipment

Alongside the legionaries, there were lighter-armed, non-citizen soldiers, called auxiliaries, such as archers from Syria and slingers from Spain. After serving for 25 years as an auxiliary, a retiring soldier would be rewarded with Roman citizenship. Roman soldiers were kept constantly busy, going on long marches carrying heavy equipment. When they were not fighting or training for war, they often had to build roads, which helped the armies move quickly from one part of the empire to another.

Sharing citizenship

The great secret of Roman success was that, unlike other ancient peoples, they were willing to share their citizenship. The right to be a Roman citizen was given not just to retiring auxiliaries, but also to the ruling classes of conquered lands, or to individuals as a reward for loyal service. This gave the conquered peoples a stake in the Roman Empire.

▼ This map shows the growth of the Roman Empire from AD 14 until 117, when it reached its largest size. For the only time in history, all these different lands were united under the rule of one people.

▶ This carving, from a triumphal arch at Carpentras in Gaul (France), commemorates campaigns against the Germans and Dalmatians in 13–9 BC. The fact that it was built in Gaul shows that the local people had come to see themselves as Romans.

Slavery

Carvings celebrating Roman victories often show defeated enemies in chains. Their fate would be slavery, to be bought and sold as property, and forced to work in quarries and mines and on farming estates. When we look at a Roman building, such as a temple, we should remember that the stones used to make it were often quarried by slaves, captured in warfare, working long hours in terrible conditions.

Roman Empire from AD 14 to 117
- Roman Empire AD 14
- Territory at its largest extent, AD 117

Civil wars

The republican system broke down in the 1st century BC, when a series of **ambitious** generals used their armies to take control of the state. For men like Julius Caesar and his rival, Pompey, to be consul for a year was no longer enough. They wanted lasting power.

Caesar and Pompey

In 49 BC, Julius Caesar, the conqueror of Gaul (France), quarrelled with Pompey, who dominated the Senate. When Pompey ordered Caesar to disband his army and return to Rome, Caesar refused. **Civil war** erupted. Caesar led his army into Italy and seized power. Pompey with the rest of the senators fled east to gather his forces. Caesar pursued them and, in 48 BC, defeated Pompey, who was later murdered. Caesar now began to behave like a king, issuing coins with his own portrait on, an honour previously only given to dead Romans. In 44 BC, he was murdered by a group of 60 senators, desperate to save the republic.

◀ Pompey was a plump man with a round face, who looked nothing like Alexander the Great. This did not stop him imitating the famous king, as this bust shows.

This hairstyle, copied from Alexander the Great, was called anastole *in Greek*

Pompey tilts his head to one side, a gesture often adopted by Alexander the Great in busts

▶ Copies of busts of Alexander the Great could be seen all over the Roman Empire. Alexander's face would have been as familar to people then as any film star is to us today. Note the brushed-up central forelocks, copied by Pompey.

Imitating Alexander

The great role model for Roman generals was King Alexander the Great of Macedonia, who had conquered a vast empire in the 4th century BC, before dying at the age of just 32. As a young man, Julius Caesar wept at the sight of a statue of Alexander, which reminded him of how little he had achieved in comparison with him. Caesar's rival, Pompey, modelled himself on Alexander. Following his conquest of Syria, Pompey was given the right to call himself 'the Great', like Alexander, and statues show that he even adopted Alexander's hairstyle, with locks brushed high from the forehead, like a lion's mane.

Octavian and Antony

Caesar's great-nephew and adopted son, Octavian, and his friend Mark Antony then seized power in Rome. After defeating Caesar's killers in battle, they shared the Roman Empire between them, with Antony ruling the east and Octavian the west. It was not long before Antony and Octavian also fell out. In 31 BC, Octavian defeated Antony and his partner, Cleopatra, queen of Egypt, at the sea battle of Actium. Antony and Cleopatra both killed themselves, leaving Octavian the sole ruler of the Roman world.

The first emperor

In 27 BC, Octavian announced that he was restoring power to the Senate. He claimed that from that time on, he would simply be Rome's *princeps* (first man). Although this gesture won him popularity, he did not give up any real power. He decided who could become a senator or consul, and he kept control of the armies. Renamed Augustus ('the honoured one'), he had become Rome's first emperor. People were grateful to Augustus for bringing peace after years of civil war. During his reign, lasting for more than 40 years, the Romans got used to being ruled by one man.

▼ This silver coin of Julius Caesar was issued in 44 BC, the year of his murder.

The Senate gave Caesar the right at all times to wear a laurel wreath, previously only worn by generals in triumphal processions. He was delighted by this, for it allowed him to hide his baldness

This type of silver coin is called a denarius

Roman coin portraits were often unflattering. Here no attempt is made to hide the lines on Caesar's scrawny neck

15

The image of Augustus

Augustus wanted people to think of him as the protector of the empire, who had brought peace after years of bitter civil war, and who was favoured by the gods of Rome. He saw that the best way to get this message across was through art.

Although Augustus ruled the empire for 44 years, his statues and coin portraits always showed him as a handsome young man. In these statues he appears in various roles. Sometimes he is a general giving commands and at other times a priest, his head covered as a sign of respect for the gods. Sometimes, he appears semi-naked, following the Greek tradition of representing god-like heroes in this way.

The Prima Porta Augustus

The most famous statue of Augustus was found in 1963 at Prima Porta, to the north of Rome. Augustus is dressed as a general wearing a decorated breastplate, at the centre of which a man hands over a standard to a Roman soldier. He comes from Parthia, a powerful eastern kingdom. The scene celebrates a treaty which Augustus made in 20 BC with the Parthians, in which they agreed to return standards they had captured following a victory over Rome, in 53 BC. Augustus claimed that he had forced the Parthians to return the standards and turned the earlier defeat into a great victory. Around this scene the gods watch approvingly.

▼ The Prima Porta statue of Augustus, carved from marble, stands 2.03 m high.

A Parthian returns one of the captured standards

Shoulder clasps decorated with mythical creatures called sphinxes. Augustus used a sphinx on his seal

The earth goddess holds a cornucopia (horn of plenty) filled with fruit. This shows that Augustus has provided peace and plenty to the empire

Cupid, son of Venus, goddess of love, riding a dolphin

In art, bare feet, like nakedness, were signs of a god-like hero

The artist has made a wonderful job in carving the military commander's cloak, or paludamentum

By Augustus' right foot, there is a figure of Cupid, the son of Venus, goddess of love. Cupid rides a dolphin, which recalls Venus' birth from the sea. This is a reminder of Augustus' claim that his own family was descended from Venus.

Augustus

We can compare the statue of Augustus with a description of him by his biographer, Suetonius:

'Augustus' eyes were clear and bright, and he liked to believe that they shone with a sort of divine radiance ... His teeth were small, few and decayed; his hair yellowish and rather curly; his eyebrows met above the nose ... His body is said to have been marred by blemishes of various sorts ... and a number of hard dry patches suggesting ringworm.'

Coins

Augustus used his coins as miniature newspapers, to announce his achievements and spread information. One side carried his portrait, together with his titles, such as 'Pater Patriae' (father of the country). The reverse had a picture, which might show a newly completed temple, with a short slogan. Typical slogans are: 'He restored the laws and rights of the Roman people', and: 'Roads have been built'.

▲ This gold coin of Augustus shows his grandsons, Gaius and Lucius, whom he adopted as his sons and heirs. He intended them to rule after him, and used coins to get people used to the idea.

▼ The Ara Pacis is an altar to the goddess of peace, built in 13–9 BC by Augustus to show that he had brought peace after the long civil wars

This badly damaged panel once showed Romulus and Remus with their father Mars and the shepherd who found them with the she-wolf

*The interior is decorated with garlands and ox skulls, representing **sacrifice** to the gods*

Aeneas, a legendary ancestor of Augustus, sacrifices a sow to the Penates, the gods who watched over Latium. Aeneas had just reached Latium after fleeing the city of Troy, sacked by the Greeks

Mars, god of war

Faustulus, the shepherd

The lower level is richly decorated with intertwined acanthus plants in full flower, as well as birds, small animals and insects. This shows that even nature is flourishing thanks to Augustus' wise rule

The city of Rome

By the 1st century AD, Rome was the world's largest city, with a population of more than a million people. Its centre was filled with grand public buildings, including temples, theatres, **amphitheatres**, race tracks, and **basilicas** (halls used as law courts and for public meetings). There were also dozens of big public bath houses. Every Roman saw this city as the centre of the world.

▲ Here you can see what remains of the Emperor Caracalla's vast bath house in Rome. This is one of the bath's great halls, which would once have been crowded with Romans relaxing and admiring art.

▼ In bath houses all over the empire, a common subject for mosaics was the sea-god Neptune. This one comes from Besançon in France.

Neptune can be identified by his trident (three-pronged fishing spear)

Real horses pull his chariot. In many mosaics, it is pulled by hippocampi (fish-tailed horses)

A dolphin, with its beak-like nose

In each corner, there is a hippocampus, a mythical creature, part-horse and part-fish

Bath house

One of the largest of Rome's bath houses was built by Caracalla, who was emperor from AD 211 to 217. It covered 11 hectares and could hold around 1600 people at any one time. This was much more than a place to wash. Caracalla's baths included gardens, restaurants, a gymnasium for exercise, a swimming pool, a running track and libraries. The bath house was also an art gallery, its halls lined with big marble statues, mostly copies of famous Greek works. The walls were faced with beautiful multi-coloured stone panels, such as purple porphyry from Egypt. **Mosaics**, showing gods and mythical sea creatures, covered the floors.

People went to the baths in the afternoons to relax, exercise and meet friends. Caracalla built his bath house in order to make himself popular with the people of Rome. It cost very little to visit, so even the poorest **citizens** could afford to go. The emperor also wanted to leave a great monument in the city, which would outdo the bath houses of earlier emperors.

Central heating

The baths used a central heating system, called a *hypocaust*, in which hot air from a furnace was passed through spaces behind walls and beneath floors. Different rooms were heated to different temperatures. There were two types of *sudatorium* (sweating room), one using dry heat, like a sauna, the other using steam. In the warm rooms, people were massaged by slaves, who rubbed their bodies with scented oil, and scraped them clean with a metal tool called a *strigil*. There were also cold rooms, with refreshing plunge baths.

▼ Every large city needed aqueducts to bring water for the baths. This wonderfully preserved example, 900 m long, can be seen in Segovia in Spain.

Water supply

The city of Rome required a vast water supply, carried from the surrounding hills along eleven huge **aqueducts**. Water constantly flowed along the aqueducts, into the bath houses, holding tanks, street fountains, public toilets and sewers, which were continually flushed. According to the Greek writer Strabo, so plentiful was Rome's water supply that 'rivers flow through the city and the sewers'.

Practical values

Frontinus (*c.* AD 35–104) was the official responsible for maintaining Rome's water supply. He proudly contrasted the usefulness of his aqueducts with the famous tombs and temples of the Greeks and Egyptians: *'I ask you! Just compare with the vast monuments of this vital aqueduct network those useless pyramids, or the good-for-nothing tourist attractions of the Greeks.'*

At this point, the aqueduct is 35 m high

The upper level has to be at exactly the right angle to ensure a constant flow of water from the hills to the city

The use of arches allowed the Romans to build on a vast scale

It was built using large granite blocks, the best local building material

Roman architecture

'In great buildings, as well as in other things, the rest of the world has been outdone by us Romans,' boasted Pliny the Elder, a Roman writer. One reason for their ability to create great buildings was the Romans' invention of concrete, which was easy to make and use. Roman concrete was made of rubble mixed with mortar made from lime (burnt chalk or limestone), volcanic ash and water. As the mortar dried it hardened, holding the concrete together, while the rubble gave the concrete its strength. Heavy stone rubble was used in the lower parts of walls, which had to bear the most weight, while light pumice rubble was used in ceilings.

▼ The tallest building in ancient Rome was the Colosseum, a vast amphitheatre built by the Emperor Vespasian and his son, Titus, in AD 72–80. Its ruined state helps us to see how it was constructed.

The other main Roman building material was brick, **mass produced** in vast quantities. Unlike a Greek temple, built with carved stones, a typical Roman temple was made of concrete and brick. Stone was saved for the skin of the building.

Arches

Roman builders made great use of the arch, a curved structure spanning an open space. A wall using arches is as strong as a solid one, but much quicker to build. It is also lighter, so it does not require such deep foundations. Arches were used to build aqueducts and the outer walls of large theatres and amphitheatres. The Romans also invented triumphal arches, decorative gateways built as monuments and used for victory processions.

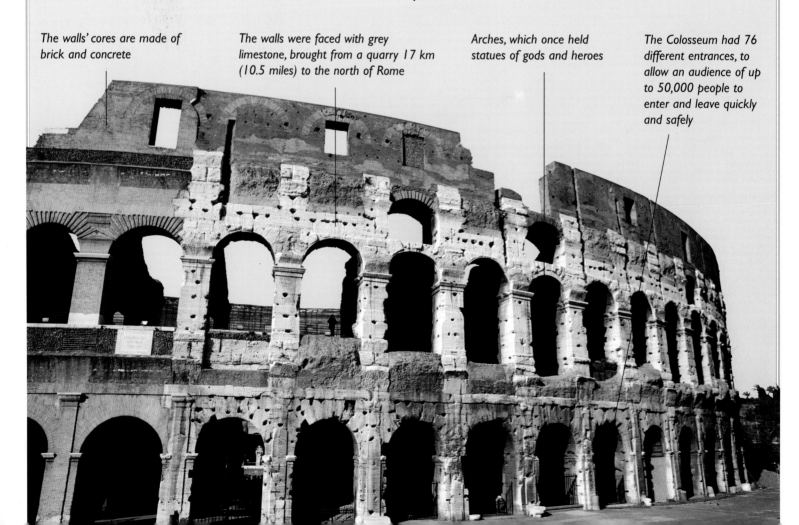

The walls' cores are made of brick and concrete

The walls were faced with grey limestone, brought from a quarry 17 km (10.5 miles) to the north of Rome

Arches, which once held statues of gods and heroes

The Colosseum had 76 different entrances, to allow an audience of up to 50,000 people to enter and leave quickly and safely

Vaults and domes

An arch could be extended to make a barrel vault (a ceiling shaped like half a cylinder). A number of arches, rotated in a circle, could also be used to make a dome, another wonderful Roman invention. For the first time, a large interior space could be created without needing dozens of columns to support the ceiling.

Slave labour

A tomb carving belonging to a family called the Haterii, who may have been building contractors, is useful evidence for construction methods. It shows the building of a large tomb resembling a temple. The scene includes a huge crane raised by men, possibly slaves, walking inside a wheel. Thanks to slavery, Roman builders had a ready supply of cheap labour, another reason for their ability to build such vast structures.

▼ This carving, from the tomb of the family of Quintus Haterius Tychicus, is one of the few Roman images of building work in progress.

These men on top of the crane show that Roman building work must have been very dangerous

Crane used to lift heavy blocks of stone

Roof covered with terracotta tiles

A portrait of the dead woman, one of the family buried in the tomb, is in the pediment, the space on a temple usually kept for statues of gods

Corinthian columns topped with Jupiter's sacred eagles

Portraits of dead members of the Haterii family

A wheel powered by men walking inside

A portrait of the dead woman shown in the temple pediment

Portraits of deceased family members

Pantheon

The most famous Roman dome is that of the Pantheon, a temple to all the gods built in Rome by the Emperor Hadrian between AD 118 and 125. It is made of concrete, with 140 square coffers (recesses). These are decorative, but also help to reduce the ceiling's weight. An opening at the top, called an *oculus* (eye), lets a beam of light stream in. Throughout the day, this beam moves around the walls, illuminating the spaces where statues of the gods once stood. Most ancient temples were designed to be seen from the outside. The Pantheon is one of the earliest buildings whose interior is even more impressive than its exterior. It has been continuously used as a place of worship ever since it was built.

Sculpture

Ancient books provide the names of dozens of sculptors who worked for the Romans. Almost all of them were Greeks, who had a long tradition of carving marble into statues and **reliefs**.

Carving

A sculptor used different tools at different stages of his work. The rough work at the beginning was done with a big hammer and heavy chisel, and a bow drill – a metal drill set spinning by a bow. For the delicate work, there were finer chisels, with flat, curved and toothed blades.

Although Roman statues seem plain today, surviving traces of paint show that they looked very different when they were made. Details, such as the eyes and hair, were brightly painted to give them a life-like appearance. They were also polished with wax, to preserve and heighten their colours.

The head is made of white Carrara marble

The lines show Caracalla as a troubled, serious man

These eyes would once have been painted

The marble has been finely polished

The emperor wears armour made from porphyry which came from Egypt

► This is a marble bust of Emperor Caracalla (ruled AD 211–17) who built the baths shown on page 18. A ruthless man, Caracalla murdered his own brother and co-ruler. He was eventually assassinated.

Marble

The most prized stone used in Roman sculpture was white marble, which has a sparkling surface and a fine grain. It could be cut into sharp details and polished to give it a smooth surface. Until the 1st century AD, marble had to be imported from Greece and Asia Minor (modern Turkey). Then the Romans discovered a new source, in the Carrara mountains of northern Italy.

Coloured marble was also used, such as porphyry, a purple stone from the Egyptian desert. In statues of emperors, sculptors might combine different marbles, using porphyry for the body, draped in a **toga** or wearing armour, and white marble for the head.

Bronze making

Bronze statues, such as those of emperors on horseback, were made by a complicated method called the 'lost wax' process. First, a sculptor made a rough clay model of the work. This was used to make a clay 'master mould'. Melted wax was then poured into the mould. After carefully removing the mould, to be used again, the wax model was given fine details. This was then encased in clay, making a second mould, which was baked, so that the wax melted and poured out through vents (holes). A pair of men used tongs to lift a **crucible** (melting pot) filled with **molten** bronze, which they poured into the mould. The bronze, which filled the space left by the 'lost wax', was then allowed to cool and harden. Finally, the mould was smashed open.

Since two men could only lift a small amount of molten bronze, statues had to be made in small pieces, which were later fitted together. Despite this, artists were able to make enormous bronze statues, called colossi. The most famous was a statue of Emperor Nero, which stood at the entrance to the emperor's palace. It was over 30 metres high, and so heavy that when it was later moved, to make way for a new temple, it required the strength of 24 elephants.

▼ This larger than life-size bronze head of the Emperor Augustus was found buried beneath the steps of a temple at Meroe in Sudan. It was probably taken there as booty by raiders, who attacked Roman Egypt in 25–21 BC.

The eyes are made of alabaster, a soft white stone, and coloured glass

The emperor tilts his head to one side. Like Pompey on page 14, he is imitating Alexander the Great

The chin shows the original colour of this bronze, which has gone green with age

Public shows

The biggest Roman buildings were those designed for public shows – circuses, or tracks, for chariot racing, and amphitheatres. An amphitheatre was a circular or oval open-air building, where men called gladiators fought to the death to entertain vast cheering crowds. These shows were staged, at great expense, by Rome's ruling classes, as a way of winning popularity.

Pictures of the shows

Art helps us to understand what went on in these buildings, and also demonstrates just how popular the shows were. All over the **empire**, people decorated their homes with mosaics and wall paintings showing gladiator fights and chariot races. The same scenes also appear on everyday items, such as vases, oil lamps and cutlery. Even babies' bottles had gladiators pictured on them. It was thought that the baby would drink in the gladiator's strength with the milk.

A favourite scene in art is the moment of victory, when one gladiator has wounded his opponent, who is no longer able to defend himself. The defeated gladiator is shown raising a finger, which meant he was asking for mercy. The crowd would then shout, 'Let him live!' or 'Finish him off!', depending on how bravely he had fought.

Although gladiators were usually slaves or criminals, they were treated like footballers or pop stars today. They had many adoring fans, who wrote **graffiti** praising their heroes, such as this line found on a wall in Pompeii: 'Celadus the Thracian makes the girls sigh'.

The mosaic may show two separate fights, or two stages of the same fight

The Latin text says, 'Astyanax conquers'

The wounded Kalendio appeals to the crowd for mercy

This symbol represents death and defeat

Kalendio has thrown his net over Astyanax

Kalendio thrusts at Astyanax's legs with his trident

The men in white are referees

◀ This Spanish mosaic records a contest between two real gladiators, called Astyanax and Kalendio. Kalendio was a *retiarus*, a fighter armed with a net and trident. Astyanax was a *secutor*, or pursuer, armed with shield and sword.

Scorpus

The poet Martial wrote a poem commemorating the death of Scorpus, the charioteer:
'I am Scorpus, the glory of the noisy Circus,
The much-applauded and short-lived
darling of Rome.
Envious Fate, counting my victories
instead of my years,
And so believing me old,
Carried me off in my twenty-sixth year'

◄ This bronze household ornament shows a chariot pulled by a team of two galloping horses. The most popular chariot races had four-horse chariots.

Executions

Mosaics show another entertainment staged in amphitheatres – public executions. Criminals were tied to stakes to be torn apart by wild beasts, such as lions and tigers. The fact that it was acceptable to decorate homes with such scenes shows how bloodthirsty Roman tastes were. People believed that it was a good thing to kill criminals, and they enjoyed watching it done.

▼ Wild beast fights were sometimes held in the circus (race track), as in this terracotta (pottery) plaque. We know that this is a race track because of the seven egg-shaped objects in the middle, used to record laps of a race.

Chariot racing

Chariot racing was almost as dangerous as fighting in the amphitheatre. Tomb inscriptions show that many charioteers died in their 20s, killed when their chariots overturned or crashed. A charioteer tied his horses' reins around his waist, so if he was thrown out of his chariot he was liable to be dragged to his death.

In the 1st century AD, the most famous charioteer in Rome was Scorpus, whose face was said to be painted on walls all over the city. Scorpus won 2048 races before he was killed, at the age of just 26.

These were lowered as each lap of a chariot race was completed

An excited spectator looks down from the safety of the front row

This man is a bestiarius, a fighter who specialized in combat with wild animals

Wild animals were often terrified by the shows, and had to be forced to fight. The lion is being driven towards the bestiarius

A dying man. The fact that he is naked suggests that he is a condemned criminal rather than a gladiator, thrown to the beasts to be executed

25

Trade and crafts

Roman rule brought peace to all the lands around the Mediterranean Sea, which was also cleared of pirates. This made it safer for merchant ships to cross the seas carrying goods, such as grain from Africa, olive oil from Spain and tin from Britain. Goods were also transported along rivers of the empire by barge.

Ships

Roman merchant ships were big-bellied vessels, with large holds, which made them stable but slow. Paintings, mosaics, coin images and carved reliefs help us to understand how they were sailed. There were two square sails that could only be used with a following wind. Images in art also show us how merchant ships were decorated, with a lucky carved figure of a goose or swan's neck and head at the stern.

A Titanic of its time

The biggest ships were those of the grain fleet. One was described by the Greek writer, Lucian:

'What a tremendous vessel it was! 180 feet [60 metres] long, as the ship's carpenter told me, and more than a quarter of this across … And how the stern rose in a graceful curve ending in a gilt goose head, in harmony with the equal curve of the bow and the forepost with its picture of Isis, the goddess who had given the ship her name. All was unbelievable: the decoration, paintings, red topsail … And the whole fortune of the ship is in the hands of a little old man who moves the great rudders with a tiller no thicker than a stick.'

▼ This crudely made black and white mosaic shows a typical merchant ship, with its two sails and steering oars.

This is the base of a Roman lighthouse

Small foresail at the prow (front)

There was one large, square mainsail

A very simple representation of a ship's figurehead, perhaps a winged goddess

The ship is steered with a pair of oars at the stern (rear). The stern rudder had not been invented

Roman glass

In the 1st century BC, glassmakers in Syria invented a new technique – glass-blowing. A glassmaker blew through an iron pipe to inflate a lump of molten glass, which was shaped by spinning and rolling. Using this technique, they could make vases with different coloured layers of glass, with a white layer on top of a dark blue layer. The outer layer was then cut away to make a relief picture called a cameo. Only thirteen complete glass cameo vases survive today. The best known is the Portland Vase, which dates from the time of Augustus (27 BC–AD 14).

Samian ware

One trade item, found on archaeological sites all over the Roman Empire, is Samian ware, a beautiful type of bright red pottery, decorated with reliefs. It was mostly made in Gaul (France), where it was mass produced in large workshops. It was manufactured by pushing clay into a stone mould, which had been carved with patterns and pictures. We know the names of many potters, which they stamped on their bowls.

◀ The Portland Vase is one of the most famous Roman works of art. The vase was intact until 1845, when it was smashed into 200 pieces by a drunk. It has been repaired three times since then. Its subject is still disputed, but it is likely that it shows the courtship of the Greek sea nymph, Thetis, by the legendary king, Pelius. Their child would be the famous hero, Achilles.

It is almost 25 cm high

The white outer layer was carefully cut away to reveal the dark blue background

The winged figure of Cupid, whose arrows cause people to fall in love

Pelius, king of Phthia in Thessally, lays hold of Thetis

The sea nymph Thetis

This may be the Greek sea god, Poseidon (Neptune), or his brother Zeus (Jupiter)

Family life

In the 2nd century AD, a Roman lawyer called Gaius wrote, 'No other peoples have such power over their children as we have.' He was talking about the power of the 'Paterfamilias' (father of the family), who headed every Roman family. The Paterfamilias had complete power over his children, daughters-in-law and grandchildren. His sons might be grown up, yet they had to wait until he died to become heads of families in their own right.

We still have many sculptures of elderly Roman men, who must have been the heads of families. These are often unflattering, with wrinkles, double chins and even warts. Even after death, a Paterfamilias remained an important family member, remembered through his portrait or through a mask of him, displayed in the home and worn at funerals.

Family masks

The Greek writer Polybius described the Roman custom of wearing masks of dead family members at funerals:

'When any distinguished member of the family dies, the masks are taken to the funeral, and are there worn by men who are considered to bear the closest resemblance to the original … It would be hard to imagine a more impressive scene for a young man who aspires to win fame and to practise virtue. For who could remain unmoved at the sight of the images of all these men, who have won renown in their time, now gathered together as if alive and breathing?'

▼ A Roman Paterfamilias, dressed in his best **toga**, proudly holds two portrait busts of his ancestors, perhaps his father and grandfather.

*Although the statue dates from the 1st century AD, he has the closely cropped hair of the **republican** period. He is an old-fashioned believer in traditional values*

The toga is beautifully carved

The figure is life-size, standing 1.65 m

Trunk of a palm tree, helping support the sculpture

◄ This richly carved relief shows a Roman marriage scene with a religious procession, on the left, and a **sacrifice**. The ceremony was overseen by a respectable older married woman, known as the *pronuba* (matron of honour)

The bride's head is covered with a flame-coloured headscarf called a flammeum

A sheep is brought to be sacrificed to the gods, to bring good luck

The man whose head is covered with his toga is the priest in charge of the sacrifice

The bride and groom join hands, watched over by the matron of honour

To be chosen to be a pronuba, a woman had to be married and still living with her first husband

Her dress was white, like those worn by many western brides today

Marriage

Marriages were arranged by the Paterfamilias of the groom and bride's families. In early times, a bride passed from her father's control to that of her husband or his father. By the 1st century BC, it was more usual for a wife to remain under the authority of her father or some other guardian. In practice, this meant that she could keep her money and property separate from her husband's.

Women

Men expected their wives to raise children, to give orders to household slaves, and to spend their spare time spinning and weaving. Even the richest women, such as Agrippina and Antonia, grand-daughters of Augustus, were taught to spin and weave.

Daughters were valued less than sons and did not even have their own names. Agrippina and Antonia were given female versions of their fathers' names, Agrippa and Mark Antony.

Despite these limitations, women could play a major role in public life. Rich women often ran their own businesses, and served in temples as priestesses. The women of the imperial family exercised great power, through their influence over their husbands and sons. One of the most powerful people in Rome was Livia, wife of Augustus and mother of Tiberius, his successor. Tiberius often complained that his mother wanted to be co-ruler of the **empire**. He could not afford to ignore her advice. She had a forceful personality and, after 52 years married to Augustus, knew everything there was to know about being an emperor.

House

On 24 August in the year 79, Mount Vesuvius, a volcano in southern Italy, erupted. Two nearby Roman towns, Herculaneum and Pompeii, were buried under a deep layer of ash, boiling mud and volcanic rocks. This terrible disaster led to the almost complete **preservation** of the two towns, which have now been uncovered by archaeologists.

Today you can visit Pompeii and Herculaneum, and walk from room to room in a Roman house. While the outside walls are plain, the inside are richly decorated with **mosaics**, wall paintings, **reliefs** made of stucco (plaster), statues and statuettes.

Atrium and triclinium

The greatest expense for a household was decorating the two most public rooms of the house, the *atrium* and the *triclinium*. The *atrium* was the entrance hall, where the family received visitors every morning. The *triclinium* was the dining room, used for dinner parties. The word *triclinium* ('three couches') comes from the Roman habit of eating while reclining on couches. Here there was often an elaborate floor mosaic, which could be admired by the diners as they ate.

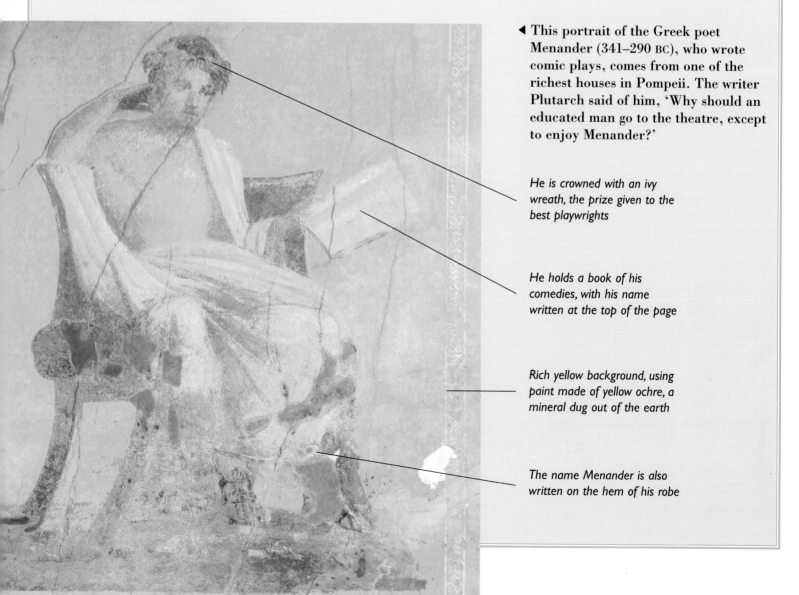

◀ This portrait of the Greek poet Menander (341–290 BC), who wrote comic plays, comes from one of the richest houses in Pompeii. The writer Plutarch said of him, 'Why should an educated man go to the theatre, except to enjoy Menander?'

He is crowned with an ivy wreath, the prize given to the best playwrights

He holds a book of his comedies, with his name written at the top of the page

Rich yellow background, using paint made of yellow ochre, a mineral dug out of the earth

The name Menander is also written on the hem of his robe

▶ This beautiful wall painting comes from a room in a house in Pompeii. It shows a nightingale singing in a garden full of flowers.

Wall paintings

Experts have identified different styles of wall painting, showing how fashions changed between 80 BC and AD 79. The earliest paintings imitate slabs of coloured marble and other types of stone. Then architectural features were added, such as columns with painted shadows, creating an illusion of depth. The next stage was to add realistic paintings of landscapes between and behind the columns. In the last style, the architectural features became purely decorative. No attempt was now made to make columns which looked like real columns.

Fashion was continually changing, which shows the importance of the home as a place to display wealth and good taste. Subjects of wall paintings were chosen for the same reasons. Paintings and mosaics of famous writers, such as the Greek playwright Menander and the Roman poet Virgil, showed a visitor how well educated the family was.

Gardens

The Romans loved gardens, and had garden scenes, with spring flowers and birds, painted on the inside walls of their homes. In the depths of winter, this was a reminder of the spring. Garden walls were also painted with outdoor scenes, to make the gardens look bigger.

A tiny dot of white makes the nightingale's eye shine

A laurel (bay) tree, sacred to Apollo

Red roses

Michaelmas daisies

Gardener's world

The writer Pliny the Younger wrote a letter to a friend in which he lovingly described the garden of his country house:
*'In front of the **colonnade** is a terrace laid out with box hedges clipped into different shapes ... with figures of animals cut out of the box ... In front is an ornamental pool, a pleasure both to see and hear, with its water falling from a height and foaming white when it strikes the marble ... Everywhere there is peace and quiet, which adds as much to the healthiness of the place as the clear sky and pure air.'*

Mosaics

The best known Roman art form is the mosaic – a picture made from tesserae, tiny pieces of pottery, stone, shell or glass, set into mortar. While few Roman paintings outside Pompeii and Herculaneum have survived, we can still see thousands of mosaics, from all over the Roman Empire. The reason is that mosaics were used on floors, which are often the only part of a Roman building to survive. Mosaics were also made to last. Before laying their tesserae, the craftsmen made sure that the floor had a firm foundation, using layers of rubble, crushed tile and mortar, pounded until the floor was level.

How were they made?

Simple patterns were made by placing tesserae directly into wet mortar. Complicated pictures were usually made in advance, either in a mosaic workshop or on the site. The tesserae might be laid in a tray of sand before a piece of glued cloth was placed on top. The whole picture was then lifted and placed onto the mortar. Once this had set, the cloth was soaked and peeled away. Gaps between the tesserae were filled, and the mosaic was cleaned and polished. In another method, the tesserae were glued directly on to the cloth, on which the picture had first been drawn, in reverse.

The mosaic includes more than 1,500,000 tiny tesserae

Alexander's horse was called Bucephalus (Ox head), from its large head

A forest of tall Macedonian pikes surrounds the king, who is being attacked from all sides

Darius appears frozen in horror, his arm outstretched towards the Persian whom Alexander has just killed

Darius's charioteer frantically whips the horses, to escape from the battlefield

The whole picture is 2.7 m by 5.2 m

Alexander is spearing a Persian nobleman, but his eyes are fixed on Darius, his true quarry

As his horse tumbles beneath him, the Persian is run through with Alexander's spear

The picture wonderfully captures the confusion and terror of a battlefield

◀ The 'Alexander mosaic' from Pompeii shows the turning point of the Battle of Issus in 333 BC. Alexander the Great charged straight for the Persian king, who fled from the battlefield.

Patterns and pictures

Similar pictures and patterns appear in mosaics from different countries. This suggests that the craftsmen may have had catalogues, with pictures of mosaics, to show to their clients for them to choose from. People could also select a mosaic reproduction of a famous painting. A 1st century AD mosaic from Pompeii shows a battle between Alexander the Great of Macedonia and King Darius of Persia. This is a copy of a lost wall painting, made around 300 BC by a Greek artist called Philoxenos.

A famous mosaic

Pliny the Elder described an unusual mosaic, which became a tourist attraction:

'The most celebrated worker in mosaic was Sosus, who at Pergamum laid the floor of what is known in Greek as the Asaraton Oecon ('Unswept Room') because, by means of small cubes tinted in various shades, he represented on the floor refuse from the dinner table and other sweepings, making them appear as if they had been left there.'

▼ A mosaic showing three birds drinking from a bowl of water, eyed from below by a hungry cat.

A pheasant

A dove, in reality much smaller than the other two birds

A ring-necked parakeet, with lovely green and red feathers

Birds and water

A popular subject for mosaics was birds, often shown drinking from a bowl of water. The writer Pliny the Elder described a mosaic by an artist called Sosus of Pergamum, which depicted 'a dove, which is drinking and casts the shadow of its head on the water, while others are sunning and preening themselves on the brim of a large drinking vessel.'

The challenge for the artist was to make water look like water

This cat may be a young leopard

Burying the dead

Some Romans believed in an afterlife, though there were different ideas about exactly where it was located. Some thought that the spirits of the dead remained near their graves, while others believed that they travelled to an underworld, deep in the earth.

Tomb carvings

Every Roman hoped to be remembered after death. Members of the ruling classes would be remembered thanks to the statues of them, set up in public places. However, ordinary people had only one place where they could display their portrait in public – on their tombs. Some tombs have carved portraits of the dead, while others have reliefs showing scenes from their lives. Such reliefs include bakers making bread, a midwife helping at a birth, and mothers with their children. Like photographs today, these carvings helped surviving relatives remember their loved ones. They also give us some of our best evidence for daily life in ancient Rome.

▼ This carving comes from the tomb of a midwife, and shows her helping a rich woman give birth. This is a work in which birth and death are linked together.

The carving shows us that Roman women gave birth in a seated position

The new mother gazes at her baby

Household slaves with towels stand by

The midwife is the only figure looking out of the picture at the viewer. This identifies her as the subject of the scene. It is as if she is saying to a passer by, 'This was my life'

The hefty-sized baby looks back up at its mother

Visiting the dead

The dead were buried in tombs outside the walls of towns, usually placed alongside the main roads, where they could be easily seen by passers-by and visited by relatives. Family members visited the grave on the dead person's birthday, and during an annual festival of the dead, called Feralia, held in late February. They brought flowers, food and wine, which were offered as gifts to the spirits of the dead. The poorest Romans, who could not afford a tomb carving, often marked a grave with the neck of a pottery jar, placed in the earth. Wine was poured into the jar for the spirit, down in the underworld, to drink.

In Egypt, there was an ancient belief that a dead person's body had to be preserved, as a mummy wrapped in bandages, for the spirit to survive. Roman mummies from Egypt were given beautiful portraits of the dead person, painted on boards which were tied in place with linen cloth. These pictures, which have survived thanks to the dry desert air, are the finest ancient portrait paintings still in existence.

▶ This is one of the mummy portraits from Roman Egypt. What we do not know is whether it was painted while its subject was still alive or after death. What do you think?

Epitaphs

Tombs were often carved with an epitaph, writing addressed to a passer-by, which described the dead person. Women's epitaphs show us the qualities that Roman men prized in their wives. The following epitaph is from a Roman tomb of the 2nd century BC:

'Visitor, what I have to say is not much, stand a moment and read. This tomb is not beautiful, but it is for a beautiful woman. Her parents gave her the name Claudia. She loved her husband with her whole heart. She bore two children, of whom she left one above ground, and buried the other beneath the earth. Her conversation was agreeable, her bearing pleasing. She stayed at home, she worked at her wool. I have finished speaking. You may go.'

Large expressive eyes are typical of these mummy portraits

She is probably wearing make-up. Roman women whitened their skin with cosmetics made from lead, not realizing that it was poisonous

The artist painted on wood with encaustic paint (pigments mixed with beeswax)

Mummy portraits are good evidence for Roman jewellery, such as this woman's earrings and necklace

Roman religion

The Romans believed in hundreds of different gods, each responsible for different areas of life. The most important was Jupiter 'Best and Greatest', the sky god. He was the special protector of the Roman **Empire**, and the emperor was his chief priest. It was the emperor's responsibility to offer prayers and gifts to Jupiter, to ensure his continued good will.

Sacrifice

Carved **reliefs** give us our best evidence for religious ceremonies. Here you can see Emperor Marcus Aurelius, whose statue on horseback we saw on page 6. The building in the background is the Temple of Jupiter on Rome's Capitoline Hill. Behind its closed doors there was a huge seated statue of the god, made of terracotta. Its great size conveyed the god's superhuman nature.

Marcus Aurelius is shown scattering incense onto a brazier, while saying a prayer which included the words, 'Keep safe the state of the **citizens**, the people of Rome.' The boy in the middle plays a pipe, in order to prevent Jupiter hearing any words except the emperor's prayer. The bull standing behind will shortly be **sacrificed** – killed as an offering to Jupiter. The killing will be done by the man who is stripped to the waist and carries an axe. Some of the bull's meat will then be burned on an altar, the rising smoke thought to carry the gift to the god.

▼ Rome's Temple of Jupiter has not survived, so this carved relief of a sacrificial scene is useful evidence for what it looked like. You can see from the column tops that it was a Corinthian temple.

Bull to be sacrificed

Marcus Aurelius, head covered, acting as a priest

Brazier for burning sweet-smelling incense, another gift for the god

Boy piper

The sacrificer, holding his axe ready

The last stage of the ceremony was to examine the bull's liver. A healthy-looking liver was believed to be a sign that Jupiter was pleased with the sacrifice, and would answer the emperor's prayers. An emperor was expected to perform this ceremony before beginning any major undertaking, such as starting a war or building a new temple. The Romans firmly believed that nothing could be achieved without the help of their gods.

Vesta's priestesses

While male gods were served by male priests, female gods had priestesses. It was the duty of the priestesses of Vesta, goddess of the hearth, to keep a sacred fire burning, day and night. Priestesses of Vesta were forbidden to marry, yet they had many privileges, such as the best seats at public shows.

Household gods

Just as there were gods who protected the Roman Empire, every house and family had its own protective household gods. These included the Lares, who watched over the dividing lines between one household and another, and the Penates, who guarded the storerooms. Entrances to homes were the responsibility of three separate gods: Forculus, who protected the doors; Limentinus, who guarded the threshold; and Cardea, goddess of door hinges. The family made daily offerings of food and wine to small statues of their household gods.

▶ This is a household shrine, like a miniature temple, where the family kept the small statues of the gods who protected their home.

▼ This relief shows the goddess Vesta, with four of her priestesses and an unidentified male figure.

Priestesses

*The **toga** tells us that this is a man, perhaps an emperor or important priest*

Vesta

Emperor worship

One strange aspect of Roman religion was that emperors were given **divine** honours, with their own temples, priests and sacrifices. People made offerings to the genius (life force) of the living emperor, while some emperors, such as Augustus, were declared to have become gods after death. Few people believed that an emperor was a god in the same way that Jupiter was. They did not expect him to answer their prayers. Rather, emperor worship was a way of showing loyalty to the Roman state.

Attitudes to being worshipped

Different emperors had different attitudes to emperor worship. Caligula (ruled AD 37–41), who was mentally ill, seems to have thought that he really was a god. According to his biographer, Suetonius, he liked to dress as Jupiter, with a golden beard and a thunderbolt, and stand in a temple, like a statue, to be worshipped. In contrast, a later emperor, Vespasian (ruled AD 79–81), made a famous joke on his deathbed, 'Dear me! I seem to be turning into a god!'

Becoming a god

The beautifully carved ivory panel on the left, dating from around AD 400, shows a funeral ceremony called a *consecratio* (making sacred), in which an emperor was thought to become a god. In the background you can see the emperor's funeral pyre, a tall wooden structure, covered with purple cloth. On top there is a statue of a four-horse chariot, the type driven by generals in triumphal processions. This represented the emperor's victory over death.

◀ This little ivory, just 30 cm by 11 cm, is one of the very last images to be made showing the old Roman religion. When it was carved, most Romans had become Christian.

A big statue of the emperor, now a god, sits in his temple on top of the carriage

The two images of the eagle suggest its flight up from the pyre

Elephants pull a great carriage in the funeral procession

In early times, the body of the emperor was placed in the pyre, though later a wax image was used instead, so that people did not have to hunt though the ashes for the emperor's bones to place in his tomb. The pyre was set alight, and an eagle was released from the topmost level. Its soaring flight represented the emperor's spirit flying up to join the other gods.

▼ This stone relief, showing Antonius Pius and his wife, Faustina, decorates one side of the base of a column, now lost. It shows us how the Romans imagined their emperors turning into gods.

Sceptre topped with Jupiter's eagle

Eagles, representing the souls of the dead couple

Antonius Pius and Faustina

Roma, goddess of the city

Figure holding an Egyptian obelisk represents the area called the Campus Martius (Field of Mars)

Romulus and Remus are carved on the shield

A winged god carries the couple up to heaven

Up to heaven

Empresses as well as emperors were sometimes deified (made into gods). On the death of his wife Faustina, in AD 141, Emperor Antonius Pius (ruled 138–161) declared that she was a goddess and built a temple in her honour. When he died, twenty years later, the temple was rededicated to both Antonius Pius and Faustina.

The emperor's successor, Marcus Aurelius, set up a relief carving (seen above) of the married couple, now gods, flying up to heaven. They are carried by a winged figure and accompanied by two eagles, while two figures on the ground watch approvingly. The seated woman on the right has a shield decorated with a carving of Romulus and Remus, with their she-wolf. This tells us that she is Roma, goddess of the city of Rome. The man on the left holding an obelisk (an Egyptian column) represents an area called the Campus Martius, where an obelisk like this stood. It was in the Campus Martius that imperial funerals took place.

New gods

As their empire grew, the Romans came across many foreign gods, most of whom were welcomed into the Roman religion. A number of eastern gods, including Isis, from Egypt, and Mithras, from Persia (Iran), were worshipped in secret ceremonies. In order to take part, people underwent rites in which they were 'initiated' (brought into the religion). Initiates had to make solemn promises never to reveal their ceremonies to outsiders.

Mystery religions, as they are called, offered people a more emotional religious experience than that provided by traditional Roman religion. Many used music and dance or a shared sacred meal, which brought the worshippers closer to their god.

The Golden Ass

In a comic novel *The Golden Ass*, the writer Apuleius mockingly described a procession by Isis worshippers: *'The horn player struck up and they started brandishing enormous swords and maces and leaping about like maniacs ... Every now and then they would bite themselves savagely and ... cut their arms with the sharp knives that they carried. One of them let himself go more ecstatically than the rest. Heaving deep sighs from the very bottom of his lungs, as if filled with the spirit of the goddess, he pretended to go stark-mad.'*

▼ This wall painting from Pompeii shows Isis worshippers holding a ceremony in a garden in front of a temple.

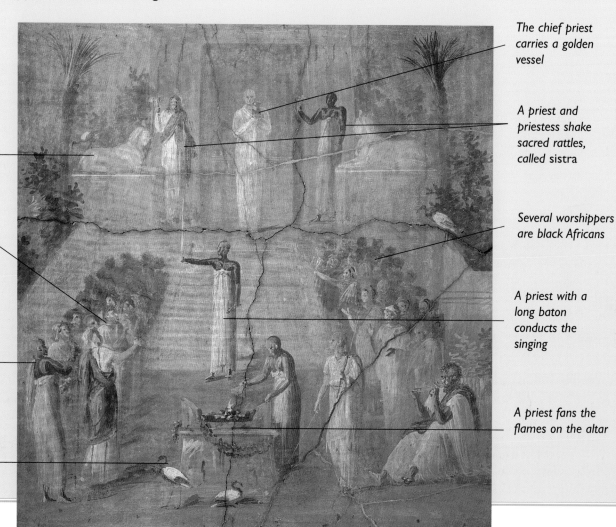

The chief priest carries a golden vessel

A priest and priestess shake sacred rattles, called sistra

Egyptian sphinxes, lions with human heads

Several worshippers are black Africans

The worshippers, wearing white linen robes, sing hymns praising their goddess

A priest with a long baton conducts the singing

Priests of Isis shaved their heads, following the ancient Egyptian custom

A priest fans the flames on the altar

Ibises, birds sacred to Isis

Mithras

Since the ceremonies of mystery religions took place in secret, art often provides our only source of evidence for them. Much of what we know of Mithras worship comes from more than a thousand pieces of sculpture, found across the empire. The commonest are carvings of the god in the act of killing a bull with a dagger. According to one view, by killing this bull, Mithras gave life to the earth. Another idea is that the figures represent constellations in the night sky. Whatever this sculpture means, it occupied the most important place in every 'Mithraeum', the dark hall where the god's initiates met to perform their mysterious ceremonies.

Christ

Christianity was another eastern religion, which spread across the empire in the 1st and 2nd centuries AD. Christians worshipped Jesus Christ, a Jewish religious teacher executed by crucifixion (being nailed to a cross) in about AD 30. They believed that Jesus was the Son of God, who had risen from the dead and who promised eternal life to his initiates.

Crucifixion was a painful and humiliating death reserved for slaves and rebels. The idea of worshipping someone who had been crucified baffled most Romans. From the emperor's point of view, the problem with Christians was their refusal to worship any Roman gods. Their failure to pay divine honours to the emperor was seen as treason. So Christians were often harshly persecuted, and thrown to wild beasts in **amphitheatres** around the empire.

▼ This dark underground room is one of a dozen Mithraea found in Rome. It is thought to represent a sacred cave, where Mithras killed the bull.

Mithras worshippers sat on these long benches at the sides, eating a sacred meal

The carving of the bull slaying is in the centre

Mithraea are always small, suggesting a limited number of worshippers

Christianity

In the early 4th century AD, there was another series of **civil wars**, eventually won by Constantine, who was sole emperor from 324 until 337. Constantine was a Christian, a follower of the religion forbidden by earlier emperors. He used his power to spread his religion, appointing Christians to important government posts, and building grand churches. He also created a new Christian capital for the empire, Constantinople.

Most of the emperors who followed Constantine were also Christians, and they made it more and more difficult to worship the old Roman gods. Under Theodosius (ruled 379–95), Christianity became the only permitted religion. Across the empire, Christians destroyed the old statues of the gods, which they believed to be devils, and carved crosses on temple walls. Many temples were torn down, while others were converted into churches.

▶ This is the church of Hagia Sophia, now a museum in Istanbul.

Light streams through 40 arched windows, which form a corona (crown)

Arabic text with the names of Allah and Muhammad, added when Constantinople was conquered by the Muslim Turks

The central dome is 31 m across and 56 m high

The dome is supported by arches

Hagia Sophia

Unlike a temple, designed as a backdrop for open-air ceremonies, a church was a building for group worship. So the interior of a church was more important, and more richly decorated, than its exterior.

The greatest late Roman church is Hagia Sophia (Holy Wisdom) in Constantinople, built by Emperor Justinian in AD 532–37. It was described by the writer Procopius as a sight of 'indescribable beauty ... full of light and sunshine'.

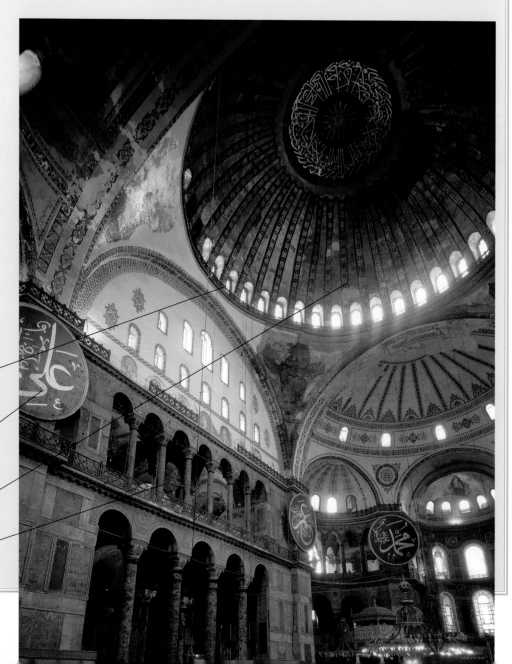

A Roman Christ

Although the old Roman religion was destroyed, Christianity took on many of its features. The role of different gods was now played by saints. Instead of asking help from a goddess, such as Diana or Minerva, worshippers turned to Mary, the mother of Christ.

This 6th-century **mosaic** from Ravenna in Italy shows Christ wearing the purple toga of an emperor, with a gold *clavus* (stripe) on his tunic. In fact, Christ was not even a Roman citizen, and would not have been entitled to wear a toga. As a Jewish man, he would have been bearded, though the mosaic shows him clean-shaven, like a late Roman. He has a circle of light around his head, called a halo, borrowed from images of the sun god, Sol Invictus. Within the halo, there is a cross, no longer thought of as a shameful image, but now the sacred symbol of the faith.

The end of Rome

By the time that Hagia Sophia was built, the old Roman Empire had broken up, as the West was overwhelmed by waves of invasions. Justinian ruled an eastern empire, which we call Byzantine. Although the empire fell, Roman traditions were kept alive by the Church, which converted the invaders to Christianity. Today, the pope (the bishop of Rome, and head of the Roman Catholic Church) still wears robes based on late Roman dress, and is called the Pontifex Maximus, the old title of Rome's chief priest.

▼ We do not know what Jesus Christ looked like, but he certainly did not resemble the clean-shaven Roman dressed in an imperial toga shown in this mosaic from a church in Ravenna in Italy.

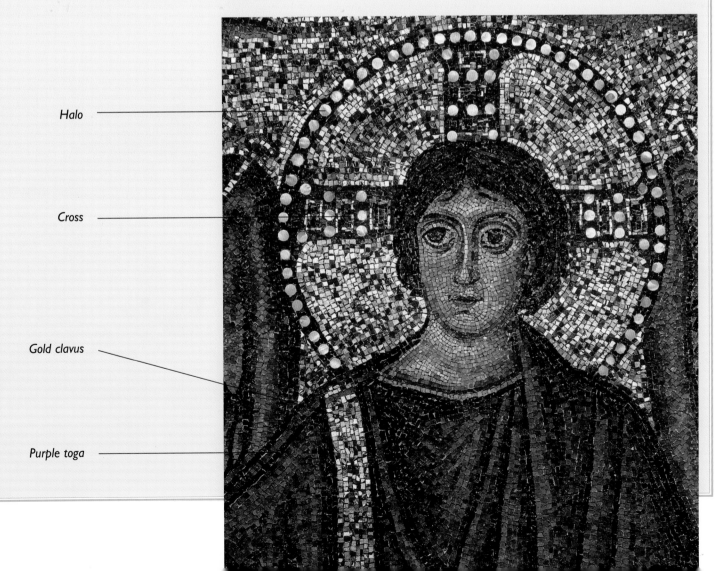

Halo

Cross

Gold clavus

Purple toga

Timeline

753 BC
date of the foundation of Rome, according to legend

510 or 509 BC
last king expelled. Rome becomes a republic

270 BC
Rome dominates all Italy

264–241 BC
First Punic War (war with Carthage)

241 BC
Rome rules Sicily

218–201 BC
Second Punic War

197–146 BC
Romans conquer Greece

149–146 BC
Third Punic War. Carthage destroyed

88 BC
first **civil war**, between Sulla and Marius

58–49 BC
Caesar conquers Gaul (France) and leads two expeditions to Britain

c.50 BC
glass-blowing invented in Syria

Carrara marble quarries opened in northern Italy

49–48 BC
civil war between Caesar and Pompey

44 BC
Caesar assassinated

33–31 BC
civil war between Octavian and Mark Antony

27 BC
Octavian, now called Augustus, becomes first Roman emperor

c. AD 30
death of Jesus Christ

AD 43
Romans conquer Britain

AD 79
Vesuvius erupts, burying Pompeii and Herculaneum

AD 80
Colosseum opened in Rome

AD 98–117
reign of Trajan. Empire reaches largest size

AD 118–25
building of the Pantheon

AD 122
Hadrian's wall begins to be built across Britain

AD 216
baths of Caracalla completed

AD 306–337
reign of Constantine, Rome's first Christian emperor

AD 330
Constantine founds new capital, Constantinople

AD 392
worship of old Roman gods banned

AD 410
Rome sacked by Visigoths (invading nomads)

AD 476
last western emperor overthrown

AD 532–7
Justinian builds the church of Hagia Sophia

AD 1453
Turks capture Constantinople

Glossary

ambitious strong desire to achieve something, such as fame or power

amphitheatre oval or circular building with rising tiers of seats around an open space, called the arena. Amphitheatres were first built by the Romans for gladiators and wild beasts to fight in.

aqueduct raised, artificial channel for carrying water

archaeology the study of past societies through their remains, such as buildings, tools and other artefacts (objects made by people)

architecture style and way of building

barbarian term for a foreigner, used by both Greeks and Romans, originally because they thought that foreign languages sounded like meaningless 'bar bar' noises

basilica hall used as a law court, and for meetings

cast form molten metal into a shape by pouring into a mould

citizen member of a state with full rights, such as the right to vote in elections

civil war war fought between people of the same country

Classical to do with the ancient Greeks and Romans, especially their art, architecture and literature

colonnade row of columns

consuls the two heads of state, elected each year, under the republic. The office continued under the emperors, but solely as an honour given to leading Romans.

crucible vessel used for melting materials at high temperatures

discipline under control, trained to obedience and order

divine god-like, superhumanly excellent, gifted or beautiful

empire large area, including a number of countries, under the control of a single state

graffiti drawing or writing on a wall

magistrate government official

mass produced made in large quantities

molten become liquid by heating

mosaic picture made from tiny pieces of stone, pottery, marble or glass, set in mortar. The name comes from 'Muse', a goddess of the arts.

preservation keeping from decay, keeping safe

propaganda information spread in order to persuade

relief sculpture or pottery in which pictures stand out from their background. In sculpture, the background would be cut away. In pottery, a relief could be made using a mould.

republic state ruled by elected heads, rather than by a king or emperor

sacrifice offering made to a god, often an animal which was killed

Senate Roman government assembly made up of heads of leading families as well as ex-magistrates

standard pole with an image on top, such as a golden eagle or a silver hand, belonging to a legion or a smaller military unit. It was carried to lead soldiers into battle, and it was a symbol of Roman honour.

toga long piece of cloth worn by men. It was draped in complicated folds around the body.

Further resources

Books

Chrisp, Peter, *The World of the Roman Emperor* (Macdonald Young Books, 1999)

Connolly, Peter, *Ancient Rome* (Oxford University Press, 2001)

Connolly, Peter, *Pompeii* (Oxford University Press, 1990)

Connolly, Peter, *The Ancient City: Life in Classical Greece and Rome* (Oxford University Press, 1998)

Dunbabin, Katherine, *Mosaics of the Greek and Roman World* (Cambridge University Press, 2001)

Field, Robert, *Geometric Patterns from Roman Mosaics and How to Draw Them* (Tarquin Publications, 1993)

Langley, Andrew & Souza, Philip de, *The Roman News* (Walker Books, 1996)

Macdonald, Fiona, *100 Things You Should Know About Ancient Rome* (Miles Kelly, 2001)

Stroud, Jonathan, *Ancient Rome: A Guide to the Glory of Imperial Rome* (Kingfisher, 2000)

Websites

http://www.vroma.org/~bmcmanus/circus.html Chariot Racing

http://harpy.uccs.edu/roman/html/roman.html Roman Art and Architecture

http://wings.buffalo.edu/AandL/Maecenas/general_contents.html Maecenas: Images of Greece and Rome

http://www.fordham.edu/halsall/ancient/asbook09.html#General Internet Ancient History Sourcebook: Rome

http://cheiron.humanities.mcmaster.ca/~trajan/ Trajan's Column

http://www.unc.edu/courses/rometech/public/frames/art_set.html Roman Arts and Crafts

http://www.romans-in-Britain.org.uk/arc_roman_mosaics.htm Romans in Britain: Roman Mosaics

Places to visit

Roman Baths, Pump Room, Stall Street, Bath BA1 1LZ
(Tel: 01225 477785)
Bath and temple complex.

The British Museum, Great Russell Street, London WC1B 3DG
Many of the finest mosaics found in Roman Britain are on display in the British Museum. You can also see statues of emperors, empresses and gods, vases, coins and household items.

Fishbourne Roman Palace, Salthill Road, Fishbourne, Chichester, Sussex PO19 3QR
(Tel: 01243 785859)
A Roman palace on the south coast of Britain with large, well-preserved mosaics.

Romans in Scotland exhibition, Hunterian Museum and Art Gallery, University Avenue, University of Glasgow, Glasgow G12 8QQ
(Tel: 0141 3304221)
Exhibition of finds showing the short-lived Roman presence in Scotland.

Roman Legionary Museum, High Street, Caerleon, Gwent NP6 1AE
(Tel: 01633 423134)
Museum of the Roman Army with a huge collection of finds from Isca (Caerleon) Roman fort.

Verulamium Museum, St Michael's Street, St Albans, Hertfordshire AL3 4SW
(Tel: 01727 751810)
Museum of Roman life set in a park, with remains of the Roman town.

Index

Alexander the Great 14, 23, 33
alphabet 5
amphitheatres 18, 20, 24, 41
Antonius Pius, Emperor 39
aqueducts 19
Ara Pacis 17
architecture 4, 5, 8, 20–1
army 7, 12, 13
Augustus, Emperor (Octavian) 15, 16, 23, 29, 38

baths 18, 19
bronzes 8, 11, 23, 25
building materials 20

calendar 5
Caligula, Emperor 38
Caracalla, Emperor 18, 22
Carthage 12
census 10
chariot racing 25
Christianity 41, 42–3
citizen 10, 11, 13
civil wars 14–15, 42
Cleopatra 15
coins 5, 14, 15, 17
Colosseum 20
Constantine, Emperor 42
Constantinople 42

death and executions 25, 28, 34–5

Egypt 15, 23, 35
emperor worship 38–9

empire 4, 12–13
Etruscans 9

families 28–9

gladiators 24
glassware 27
gods 16, 27, 36–7, 40–1
government 10–11
Greek influence 8, 16

Hagia Sophia 42, 43
Herculaneum 30, 32
homes 30–1
hypocaust 19

Julius Caesar 14, 15
Justinian, Emperor 42, 43

language 4, 5
Lares and Penates (household gods) 37
Livia 29

Marcus Aurelius, Emperor 5, 6, 7, 36, 39
Mark Antony 15, 29
Mars 5, 17
Menander 30, 31
Mithraeum 41
Mithras 40–1
mosaics 18, 24, 26, 32–3

Nero, Emperor 23

Pantheon 21
Pompeii 30, 32, 33, 40
Pompey 14
Prima Porta Augustus 16

religion 36–43
republic 10–11, 14
Roma 39
Rome, city of 8, 17, 18–21, 36, 39
Romulus and Remus 8, 17, 39

Samian ware 27
Scorpus 25
sculpture 6, 7, 13, 16, 21, 22–3, 28, 34; see also bronzes
Senate 10, 14
Septimius Severus, Emperor 4
slaves 13, 21
standards 12, 16

Theodosius, Emperor 42
Tiberius, Emperor 29
Titus, Emperor 20
toga 5, 9, 11, 43
trading 26
Trajan, Emperor 7
Trajan's column 7, 12

Venus 17
Vespasian, Emperor 20, 38
Vesta 37
Virgil 9, 31

wall paintings 4, 31, 40
women 10, 29

Titles in the *History in Art* series include:

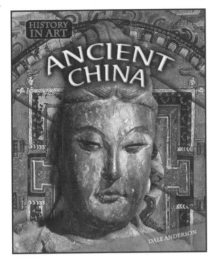

Hardback   1 844 43369 2

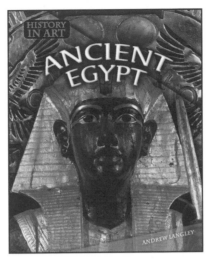

Hardback   1 844 43361 7

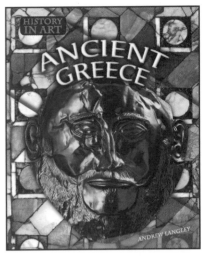

Hardback   1 844 43359 5

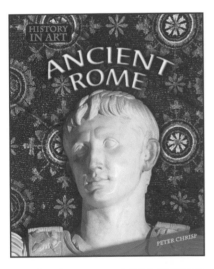

Hardback   1 844 43360 9

Hardback   1 844 43362 5

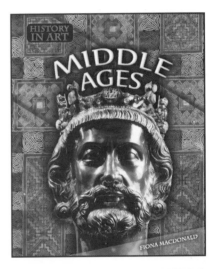

Hardback   1 844 43370 6

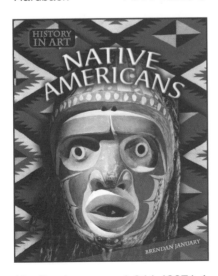

Hardback   1 844 43371 4

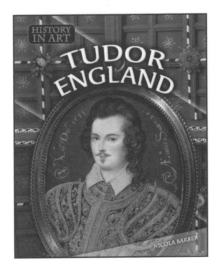

Hardback   1 844 43372 2

Hardback   1 844 43373 0

Find out about the other titles in this series on our website www.raintreepublishers.co.uk